BEI GRIN MACHT SIC
WISSEN BEZAHLT

- Wir veröffentlichen Ihre Hausarbeit,
  Bachelor- und Masterarbeit

- Ihr eigenes eBook und Buch -
  weltweit in allen wichtigen Shops

- Verdienen Sie an jedem Verkauf

Jetzt bei www.GRIN.com hochladen
und kostenlos publizieren

Bibliografische Information der Deutschen Nationalbibliothek:

Die Deutsche Bibliothek verzeichnet diese Publikation in der Deutschen National-
bibliografie; detaillierte bibliografische Daten sind im Internet über http://dnb.d-
nb.de/ abrufbar.

Impressum:

Copyright © 2015 GRIN Verlag, Open Publishing GmbH
Druck und Bindung: Books on Demand GmbH, Norderstedt Germany
ISBN: 978-3-668-07989-2

Dieses Buch bei GRIN:

http://www.grin.com/de/e-book/309320/credit-rating-agencies-what-impact-do-
they-have-and-do-we-really-need

Alexej Eichmann

Credit Rating Agencies. What Impact Do They Have and Do We Really Need Them?

GRIN Verlag

GRIN - Your knowledge has value

Der GRIN Verlag publiziert seit 1998 wissenschaftliche Arbeiten von Studenten, Hochschullehrern und anderen Akademikern als eBook und gedrucktes Buch. Die Verlagswebsite www.grin.com ist die ideale Plattform zur Veröffentlichung von Hausarbeiten, Abschlussarbeiten, wissenschaftlichen Aufsätzen, Dissertationen und Fachbüchern.

Besuchen Sie uns im Internet:

http://www.grin.com/

http://www.facebook.com/grincom

http://www.twitter.com/grin_com

Master of Business Administration (MBA)

Credit Rating Agencies

What impact do they have and do we really need them?

Module: Economics

Assignment: No. 1/1

Author: Alexej Eichmann

2015

Executive Summary

In the last few years Credit Rating Agencies have come under a lot of criticism, especially because the credit risk of structured credit products has been underestimated or has been communicated too late by CRAs which led to issues at the macro-economic level like the case of Greece in 2010 as well as at the micro-economic level like the case of Enron from 2001 or the case of Lehman Brothers from 2008 has shown.

CRAs are private, profit-oriented companies which evaluate credit risks of organizations like governments, financial or non financial institutions that issue debt in public markets. While assigning a letter grade to a bond, which represents an opinion, CRAs indirectly inform if the organization is able to pay back capital and interest in time. In an oligopoly market with a total revenue of €4,1 billion and a growth rate of 22.4% since 2010, there are three main competitors, whereas over 150 different CRAs are known. The so called "Big Three" have a share of around 95% of the market. This assignment analyses the impact of Credit Rating Agencies on the financial market focusing on corporate institutions. In the case of Enron, a former American energy, commodities and services company, it received good credit ratings up until four days before bankruptcy. Other examples like Lehman Brothers or WorldCom show, that Moody's, S&P and Fitch still rated these companies as safe investments days before their bankruptcy. Credit Rating Agencies influence about 80% of the world market capital. The industry is dominated by S&P and Moody's which lead to a lack of competition.

Ratings have an impact on the overall economic performance, recently proofed by the financial crisis caused in the US subprime mortgage market. The conflict of interest occurs from the issuer-pay model where almost all credit ratings are paid by the issuer of the instrument. CRAs are governed by the International Organization of Securities Commissions (IOSCO) which established a "Code for Conduct Fundamentals" for CRAs, a voluntary code without enforcement mechanisms.

Authorities have responded with a range of regulatory reforms. There is currently no consensus on a common set of reform. The overall rating agencies do not take any responsibility for damage caused to governments or investors.

Table of Contents

List of Abbreviations & Symbols

&	and
ABS	Asset Backed Securities
CESR	Committee of European Securities Regulators
cp.	compare
CRA	Credit Rating Agency
DBRS	Dominion Bond Rating Service
ECAI	External Credit Assessment Institution
e.g.	for example
IOSCO	International Organization of Securities Commissions
NRSRO	Nationally Recognized Statistical Rating Organizations
S & P	Standard & Poor's
SEC	Securities and Exchange Commission
US	United States

List of Tables

1 Introduction

1.1 Problem Definition and Objective

John Moody has founded the first rating agency in the US in 1909, the start for a multi-trillion dollar market.[1] Nowadays Credit Rating Agencies (CRAs) play an important role in the globalized financial markets.

Taking into consideration the Oil crisis in 1973/76, the Asian crisis in 1997 or the more recent world financial crisis in 2008, CRAs have come under a lot of criticism in the last few years. According to the opinion of many observers, the credit risk of structured credit products has been underestimated or has been communicated too late by CRAs which led to issues at the macro-economic level like the case of Greece in 2010 as well as at the micro-economic level like the case of Enron from 2001 or the case of Lehman Brothers from 2008 has shown.[2]

This work will critically review the impact and importance of CRAs on global financial systems and global economy. The impact on issuing sovereign ratings will only party be touched as the main focus is on corporations and financial institutions on capital markets. Based on the impact shown in this assignment a critical analysis will identify why CRAs are criticized and how the related issues can be solved.

1.2 Scope of Work

A brief description of the topic and objective of this assignment has been presented in this chapter. Within chapter two, basic information on the purpose and function of CRAs and the market structure of credit rating will be provided. Chapter three focus on the impact of CRAs, providing the key-facts of criticism along the case example of Enron and others. Finally the last chapter will offer a conclusion and will give an outlook on the ideas how the situation needs to be changed to solve the main issues with CRAs.

---

[1] Cp. Sylla R. (2002), p.19.
[2] Cp. de Haan J., Amtenbrink, F. (2011), p.1.

2 Background on Credit Rating Agencies

2.1 Definition, Purpose and Function

Credit rating can be defined as "an opinion regarding the creditworthiness of an entity, a debt or financial obligation, debt security, preferred share or other financial instrument, or of an issuer of such a debt [...] issued using an established and defined ranking system of rating categories".[3]

CRAs are private, profit-oriented companies which evaluate credit risks of organizations like governments, financial or non-financial institutions that issue debt in public markets. While assigning a letter grade to a bond, which represents an opinion, CRAs indirectly inform if the organization is able to pay back capital and interest in time.[4] Generally CRAs reduce the asymmetries in available information between issuer and investors while providing rating to "make it easy for investors to compare different potential investments".[5] The provided ratings do not cover all important aspects, like price volatility or market liquidity, being able to make investment decisions. This means e.g. that bonds with the same rating can have different market prices.[6]

For each rating the CRAs use own and different methodologies, tools and scales. For different sectors, asset classes[7] or geographical regions a calculation is based on different criteria (qualitative and quantitative).[8] Compared to corporate debt ratings, which are based on public available data, the data used by the CRAs for financial ratings comes from the issuer and is nonpublic and nonstandard.

In literature three main purposes of credit ratings can be found. Beside the mentioned "information service", where information asymmetries between debt issuer and investor are solved through evaluation of the ability meeting debt obligations through the issuer with the result of increasing the number of potential borrowers and promoting liquid markets, CRAs are also providing "monitoring services" where they implicitly influence issuer to take corrective actions to minimize risk of downgrades. Downgrades can destabilize financial markets through "statistically significant spillover effects across countries and financial markets"[9]. Especially through the

---

[3] European Parliament (2009), L 302/1.
[4] Cp. Financial Times Online (2014), w/o p.
[5] Langohr H., Langohr P. (2010), p.1.
[6] Cp. Katz J., Salinas E., Stephanou C. (2009), p.1.
[7] Such as corporates, financial institutions, public/structured finance, insurance companies.
[8] Cp. Alcubilla R., Ruiz del Pozo J. (2012), p.184.
[9] International Monetary Fund (2010), p.86.

"certification services" (e.g. rating of securities as investment or non-investment grade) CRAs are strongly embedded into regulatory within capital requirements (e.g. calculation of Basel II capital risk-requirements). In these ways CRAs have an impact on the demand and the market liquidity.[10]

Historically the business model of CRA's was different before the 1970s, where subscription fees for rating have been charged to investors. During this time the CRAs were less successful not playing an important role in the financial system, especially because ratings were created on publicly available data and therefore not very interesting for investors. Due to less importance the US Securities and Exchange Commission (SEC) decided not to regulate the credit rating industry but to rely on the ratings of mayor agencies and creating the concept of NRSROs (Nationally Recognized Statistical Rating Organizations)[11] in 1975. By nominating mayor CRAs for NRSRO and by establishing legal rules where companies depend on NRSRO ratings the business of rating grew significantly during 1990s.[12]

2.2 Structure of Credit Rating Process

The methodologies and processes used for ratings are different from agency to agency. Despite the various approaches, the international CRAs follow similar procedures depending on the different rating targets[13]. In general the overall rating process takes between one and two month but can differ if e.g. the complexity of the rating is high.[14]

The common rating process can be divided into five steps: Within the first step the rating is initiated on request by the issuer. In this phase a contract is signed regulating the key points of collaboration (e.g. confidentiality) between CRA and issuer. Step two includes the collection of necessary data and is either based on publicly available information or requested from the issuer. Within step three the analytical team of the CRA evaluates the collected data quantitatively and qualitatively based on their specific methods taking factors like characteristics of a country or global environment into consideration.[15] Beside the fact of having different methodologies, the main objective of the CRA is to analyze all factors affecting the creditworthiness of an issuer (cp. 2.1), which are e.g. characteristics of industry, business and finance,

---

[10] Cp. Kiff H., Nowak S., Schumacher L. (2012), p.12.
[11] See also External Credit Assessment Institution (ECAI) in the European Union.
[12] Cp. Partnoy F. (2006), p. 62-64.
[13] E.g.: companies, financial institutions, insurance.
[14] Cp. Alcubilla R., Ruiz del Pozo J. (2012), p.18.
[15] Cp. Kruck A. (2011), p. 26.

efficiency of operation or quality of management, competitive situation of the issuer or legal issues. As the credit rating is more related to specific financial instruments it includes further factors like earnings capacity of the company and their volatility, level of liquidity, financial flexibility of the company to raise funds to overcome temporal financial needs or available support from strong external sites. Having the information analyzed the committee of the CRA responsible for specific rating votes on the grade. Findings are presented to the issuer who is given the chance to comment on the rating or to provide further information which may be relevant to adjust the rating. The rating is published after the issuer has finally accepted it. The final step includes the continuous monitoring of the financial instrument during its life-time. CRAs are obliged to review the information regularly, to change the rating when necessary and to publish the new results.[16] The rating grade gives an opinion about the quality of a rated product. Ratings for securities with a runtime of less than one year are called short-term ratings and long-term ratings exceeding runtime of one year.[17] Table 1 shows the grades of the three main CRAs for long-term ratings.

S&P and Fitch	Moody's	Interpretation of grade	
AAA	Aaa	Highest Quality, reliable, stable	Investment grade
AA+, AA, AA-	Aa1, Aa2, Aa3	Quality, but a little more risk	
A+, A, A-	A1, A2, A3	Strong payment capacity	
BBB+, BBB, BBB-	Baa1, Baa2, Baa3	Adequate payment capacity	
BB+, BB, BB-	Ba1, Ba2, Ba3	Likely to fulfill obligations, ongoing uncertainty	Speculative grade
B+, B, B-	B1, B2, B3	High-risk obligations	
CCC+,CCC, CCC-	Caa1, Caa2, Caa3	Vulnerable to default	
CC, C, D	Ca, C, D	Near or in bankruptcy or default	

Table 1: Overview Long-term Credit rating grades in decreasing order of quality[18]

All grades below BB+ / Ba1 are speculative with a high risk to default, grades above are counted as investment potential with a lower risk. A high credit grade indicates a stronger credit profile and will generally result in lower interest rates charged by lenders.

2.3 Market Structure of Credit Rating Agencies

In an oligopoly market with a total revenue of €4,1 billion and a growth rate of 22.4% since 2010, there are three main competitors, whereas over 150 different CRAs are known. The so called "Big Three" have a share of around 95% of the market. Standard & Poor's Rating Services with 40%, Moody's Investors Service with 40%

---

[16] Cp. Host A. (2012), p. 645.
[17] Cp. Standard & Poor's (2012b), p. 3-6.
[18] Modified by the author according to International Monetary Fund (2010), p. 90.

and Fitch Ratings with 15%.[19] Table 2 shows the dominant market position of the "Big Three" based on the number of credit ratings per rating category. The small CRAs like DBRS[20] play de facto no role.

NRSRO	Financial Institutions	Insurance Companies	Corporate Issuers	Asset-Backed Securities	Government Securities	Total Ratings
S&P	60,300	7,600	47,400	97,500	930,500	1,143,300
Moody's	50,795	3,639	32,510	82,357	754,062	923,363
Fitch	51,718	3,786	15,367	56,311	223,188	350,370
Others	32,136	4,883	7,999	24,396	18,137	87,551
Total	194,949	19,908	103,276	260,564	1,925,887	2,504,584

Table 2: Number credit ratings per NRSRO and rating category[21]

The market barrier entries are very high for new competitors. Beside the strong regulations by SEC (Cp. 2.1) or the high dependency on available information as a business model especially the "pressure of reputation"[22] is the limiting factor for new CRAs. Most financial institutions (Demand side of market) would simply ignore new agencies thus issuer of financial instruments (Supply side of market) would do so.

---

[19] U.S. Securities and Exchange Commission (2013), p. 8.
[20] Biggest Canadian rating agency.
[21] Data Source: U.S. Securities and Exchange Commission (2013), p. 8.
[22] Utzig S. (2010), p. 10.

3 Impact of Credit Rating Agencies in the financial world

3.1 The Collapse of Enron and other examples

Credit rating changes can have significant impact on financial markets as several examples have shown. A SEC survey form 2003 found out that pension funds, insurance companies, endowments or foundations use credit ratings to comply with internal and legal policies requiring minimum credit standards. The performance of portfolio-managers is benchmarked against indices which are based on credit ratings. The Barcley Euro Bond e.g. only contains investment-grade rated instruments which are removed in case of downgrades.[23]

In the case of Enron, a former American energy, commodities and services company, it received good credit ratings up until four days before bankruptcy. Good credit ratings were important for Enron to operate and to expand its trading business as well as to access the capital markets. Even if CRAs had no relationship of interest with Enron (beside payment for service), the question was raised why CRAs did not fulfill their information and monitoring service and informed in time correctly. In August 2001 accounting adjustments in the balance sheet have been reported to CRAs, in November 2001 Enron was seeking a equity investor to address its liquidity problems. CRAs decided only to downgrade in small steps, but still above investment grade. Enron's business model depended on investment grade ratings and would have been gone bankruptcy without. Because of some issues with the possible investor Dynergy, Moody's decided to lower Enron's rating below investment grade on November 7th and informed Enron one day later about the decision. Enron tried to postpone the press release and was supported by several shareholders who expressed their concerns to Moody's. Convinced, Moody's rated down to the lowest investment grade. After several hick-ups between Enron and Dynergy, the CRA's decided finally to downgrade Enron below investment-grade on November 28th. Four days later Enron field for bankruptcy. [24]

Other examples like Lehman Brothers (2008) or WorldCom (2002) show, that Moody's, S&P and Fitch still rated these companies as safe investments days before their bankruptcy. [25]

---

[23] Cp. International Monetary Fund (2010), p. 92.
[24] Cp. Coskun D. (2008), p. 266 ff.
[25] Cp. Kingsley, P. (2012), w/o p.

It can be proved, that small up- and downgrades have only a limited impact on the default risk of loans whereas changes into or out of investment grade categories have significant impact. CRAs are powerful institutions which influence "issuer survival by affecting their access to funding markets and their funding costs"[26]. Moody's downgrades have statistically less impact on financial markets compared to Fitch and S&P due to the fact that Moody's tend to follow the others.

Taking the rating stability into consideration, CRAs tend to avoid frequent rating changes to suggest stability which is preferred by the market participants. This is important because downgrades could be interpreted by forced sale. In this regards sovereign ratings seem to be more stable than corporate ones.[27]

Ratings have an impact on the overall economic performance, recently proofed by the financial crisis caused in the US subprime mortgage market.[28] CRAs were involved in the process securitization of mortgages, fueling the "unsustainable growth" of Asset Backed Securities (ABS) which was a catalyst for the global financial crisis.[29] To regain reputation back of underestimated risk, CRAs downgraded the Eurozone states more aggressively.

3.2   Critical Analysis of CRAs

After the scandals of Enron and WorldCom the large CRAs came under intensive criticism. Related to Enron CRAs were accused for not asking sufficient questions to the company management or accessing confidential information effectively and at the end not providing timely good quality information.[30] Additionally CRAs are "lagging" behind the market changes by announcing changes not in time, resulting in a questioned reliability of CRAs.[31]

If CRAs influence the market, their ratings are important from a financial stability perspective. Would they just reflect on the market available information, their actions would not be relevant and no concerns would be raised.[32]

---

[26] Kiff H., Nowak S., Schumacher L. (2012), p. 4.
[27] Cp. Kiff H., Nowak S., Schumacher L. (2012), p. 14 ff.
[28] Cp. Setty G., Dodd R. (2003), p. 12.
[29] Cp. de Haan J., Amtenbrink F. (2011), p. 14-16 and Katz J., Salinas E., Stephanou C. (2009), p. 3.
[30] Cp. Frost C. (2007), p. 482.
[31] Cp. Baum C., Karpava M., Schäfer D., Stephan A. (2014), p. 21.
[32] Cp. Kiff H., Nowak S., Schumacher L. (2012), p. 3.

The conflict of interest occurs from the issuer-pay model where almost all credit ratings are paid by the issuer of the instrument.[33] Between $30,000 to $2.4 million for corporate debt and structured finance instruments are issued, resulting in 90% of overall revenue for CRAs.[34] Credit Rating Agencies influence about 80% of the world market capital.[35] The industry is dominated by S&P and Moody's which lead to a lack of competition. Normally two ratings are needed to issue rated debt; therefore both companies do not compete with each other. As described (cp. 1.2) due to requirements of NRSRO it is difficult for new competitors to enter the market.

It has been shown that CRAs have high impact within financial markets as an assessment tool for investors. While rating decisions are based on a defined methodology, CRAs admit their ratings are opinions and cannot be verified in courts which lead to a lack of accountability.[36] Even if the rating methodologies seem to be transparent, some market observers criticize that CRAs do not publish "verifiable and easily comparable historical performance data"[37]. CRAs do not disclose their assumptions when rating structured finance products, resulting in a lack of transparency.

CRAs are governed by the International Organization of Securities Commissions (IOSCO) which established a "Code for Conduct Fundamentals" for CRAs, a voluntary code without enforcement mechanisms. Recent past shows a need for a more legal binding regulatory framework.[38]

3.3 Learnings and regulatory solutions

Many reports have stated out the role of CRAs and the impact in the crisis. Authorities have responded with a range of regulatory reforms. There is currently no consensus on a common set of reform, but the main objectives are:

- Managing conflicts of interest through governance reforms.
- Improving quality of rating methodology.
- Increasing transparency by disclosure obligations.
- Replace self-regulation by government oversight.

---

[33] Cp. International Monetary Fund (2010), p. 94.
[34] Cp. Partnoy F. (2006), p. 68-69.
[35] Cp. Steiner H. (2009), w/o p.
[36] Cp. Ryan J. (2012), p. 8-10.
[37] IOSCO (2008), p. 9.
[38] Cp. de Haan J., Amtenbrink F. (2011), p. 17-18.

The IOSCO revised the Code of Conduct in 2008 by strengthening the quality and monitoring of the rating process as well as public disclosures and review of compensation policies. IOSCO suggested using the code as a template in all countries to avoid fragmentation. In April 2009 the G-20 leaders agreed that national authorities will enforce compliance, with the IOSCO playing a coordinating role. A regulation on CRAs was approved in early 2009 by the EU and communicated by the commission. All CRAs who would like to use their ratings in the EU need to register to the Committee of European Securities Regulators (CESR), supervised by it and the relevant member states. This includes legally binding rules going further from IOSCO code, e.g. advance disclosure and transparency requirements, stronger internal governance mechanisms or prohibition from advisory services. The CESR aims to establish a central repository for the public with historical data and performance of all registered CRAs.[39]

---

[39] Cp. Katz J., Salinas E., Stephanou C. (2009), p. 5.

4   Conclusion and Outlook

Based on the examples provided it is clear, that CRAs play across the financial sectors a critical role as "capital market gatekeepers".[40] Particularly CRAs have large influence on the capital requirements for banks and financial institutions (Basel II and III). Significant downgrades in ratings accelerate market collapse whereas good ratings can fuel the growth of markets and the economy. It is obvious that institutions are needed, solving the information asymmetries between issuer and investors.

Nevertheless the overall rating agencies do not take any responsibility for damage caused to governments or investors. The economic crisis as well as the collapse of Enron or other institutions show that CRAs are an important element of the global financial markets and therefore need an effective supervision and legal responsibility.[41]

The main issues like the lack of accountability or credibility as well as the lack of competition and transparency of the methodology and tools have been recognized by governments and regulatory institutions. Different and not united measures have been introduced, mainly focusing on reducing self-regulation of CRAs and introducing stronger governmental supervision as well as correctness and completeness of ratings.

To overcome the oligopolistic market structure with the Big Three dominating the market or to revise the issuer-pays model in this industry was less successful until now, especially as there is no easy solution to solve these problems. There are already many small players in the market, but they remain limited not gaining enough market acceptance. Promoting further competition in an issuer-pays model might have negative impact on the quality of ratings because CRAs might compete on offering better ratings or lower prices. In contrast to that, only few market players would signal consistency and comparability and could not provide security to investors.

The change of the issuers-pays model to investors-pays might look like as an easy solution in a first place, like performed until 1980s. But as CRAs strongly depend on a revenue stream it is assumed that investors are unwilling to pay the substantial subscription fee and finally this would not solve the problem but just shift it from

---

[40] Cp. Katz J., Salinas E., Stephanou C. (2009), p. 3.
[41] Cp. Host A., Cvecic I., Zaninovic V. (2012), p. 656.

issuers to investors. An idea would be to have a hybrid solution, where issuers would pay a fee to the known ratings agencies and would need a second "opinion" from an agency with a subscriber fee.[42]

Overall it is unrealistic that regulations and frameworks which require credit ratings for certain financial instruments are changed in the near future. This secures the existence of CRAs and therefore makes it necessary to change the current situation to prevent cases like the financial crisis or downfalls of companies and institutions.

---

[42] Cp. Katz J., Salinas E., Stephanou C. (2009), p. 6-7.

Bibliography

Alcubilla R., Ruiz del Pozo J. (2012): Credit Rating Agencies on the Watch List: Analysis of European Regulation, Oxford University Press, Oxford, 2012.

Baum C., Karpava M., Schäfer D., Stephan A. (2014): Credit Rating Agency Downgrades and the Eurozone Sovereign Debt Crisis, Boston College, Retrieved from: http://fmwww.bc.edu/EC-P/wp841.pdf (Accessed 25.01.2015).

Collins D. (2006): Behaving Badly - Ethical Lessons from Enron, Dog Ear Publishing, Indianapolis, USA.

Coskun D. (2008): Credit rating agencies in a post-Enron world in Journal of Banking Regulation, Vol. 9, 4 264–28, 1. August 2008, Palgrave Macmillan.

de Haan J., Amtenbrink, F. (2011): Credit Rating Agencies. DNB Working Paper No. 278 / January 2011, Amsterdam.

European Parliament, Council of the European Union (2009): Regulation (EC) No 1060/2009 of the European Parliament and of the Council of 16 September 2009 on credit rating (O.J. 2009, L 302/1). Retrieved from: http://eur-lex.europa.eu/legal-content/EN/LSU/?uri=CELEX:32009R1060 (Accessed 05.11.2014).

Financial Times Online (2014): Definition of rating agencies. Retrieved from: http://lexicon.ft.com/Term?term=rating-agencies (Accessed 05.11.2014).

Fox L. (2004): Enron - The Rise and Fall, John Wiley & Sons, Hoboken, New Jersey.

Frost C. (2007): Credit Rating Agencies in Capital Markets: A Review of Research Evidence in: Selected Criticisms of the Agencies, Journal of Accounting, Auditing & Finance, June 1st 2007.

Host A., Cvecic I., Zaninovic V. (2012): Credit rating agencies and their impact on spreading the financial crisis on the eurozone, 2012. Retrieved from: hrcak.srce.hr/file/138622 (Accessed: 20.11.2015).

International Monetary Fund (2010): The Uses and Abuses of Sovereign Credit Ratings in Global Financial Stability Report October 2010. Retrieved from: https://www.imf.org/external/pubs/ft/gfsr/2010/02/pdf/chap3.pdf (Accessed: 5.11.2014).

IOSCO (2008): The role of credit rating agencies in structured financial markets. Technical Committee of the International Organization of Securities Commissions. Retrieved from: http://www.fsa.go.jp/inter/ios/20080328/04.pdf (Accessed: 01.02.2015).

Katz J., Salinas E., Stephanou C. (2009): Credit Rating Agencies, World Bank Other Operational Studies 10227, The World Bank, Washington, 2009.

Kiff H., Nowak S., Schumacher L. (2012): Are Rating Agencies Powerful? An Investigation into the Impact and Accuracy of Sovereign Ratings, IMF Working Paper. Retrieved from: http://www.economy.gov.ae/Arabic/DocLib/IMF%20Working%20Paper_CRAs_2012.pdf (Accessed 5.11.2014).

Kingsley P. (2012): How credit ratings agencies rule the world. The Guardian, 15.February 2012. Retrieved from: http://www.theguardian.com/business/2012/feb/15/credit-ratings-agencies-moodys (Accessed: 24.01.2015).

Kruck A. (2011): Private Ratings, Public Regulations: Credit Rating Agencies and and Global Financial Governance, Palgrave Macmillan, Chippenham and Eastbourne.

Langohr H., Langohr P. (2010): The Rating Agencies and Their Credit Ratings: What They Are, How They Work, and Why They are Relevant, John Wiley & Sons, West Sussex, 2010.

Markham, J. (2006): A Financial History of Modern U.S. Corporate Scandals: From Enron to Reform, M.E. Sharpe, USA.

McKinsey & Company Inc., Koller T., Goedhart M., Wessels D. (2010). Valuation: Measuring and Managing the Value of Companies, John Wiley & Sons.

Niskanen W.A. (2007): After Enron - Lessons for Public Policy, Rowman & Littlefield Publishers, USA.

Partnoy, F. (2006): How and why credit rating agencies are not like other gatekeepers, Research Paper No. 07-46, University of San Diego, 2006.

Rapoport N. (2009), Lessons From Enron - And Why We Don't Learn From Them. Scholarly Works. Paper 123. Retrieved from http://scholars.law.unlv.edu/facpub/123 (Accessed: 14.11.2014).

Ryan J. (2012): The Negative Impact of Credit Rating Agencies and proposals for better regulation, Working Paper FG 1, January 2012 Nr. 1, SWP Berlin.

Setty G., Dodd R. (2003): Credit Rating Agencies: Their Impact on Capital Flows to Developing Countries, Special Policy Report 6, Financial Policy Forum, Washington D.C..

Standard & Poor's (2012a): Ratings Direct on the Global Credit Portal. Retrieved from: www.standardandpoors.com/ratingsdirect (Accessed: 12.11.2014).

Standard & Poor's (2012b): Standard & Poor's Ratings Definitions. Retrieved from: http://www.standardandpoors.com/spf/general/RatingsDirect_Comment ary_979212_06_22_2012_12_42_54.pdf S. (Accessed: 02.11.2014).

Steiner H. (2009) in Wagner E. (2008): Credit Swaps und Informationsgehalt, Gabler, Wiesbaden.

Sylla R. (2002): An historical primer on the business of credit rating, in: Levich R., Majnoni G., Reinhart C.(Eds.), Ratings, Rating Agencies and the Global Financial System, Springer Science & Business Media, New York, 2002.

U.S. Securities and Exchange Commission (2013): Annual Report on Nationally Recognized Statistical Rating Organizations. Retrieved from: http://www.sec.gov/divisions/marketreg/ratingagency/nrsroannrep1213.pdf (Accessed: 09.11.2014).

Utzig S. (2010): The Financial Crisis and the Regulation of Credit Rating Agencies: A European Banking Perspective. Retrieved from: http://www.adbi.org/files/2010.01.26.wp188.credit.rating.agencies.european.banking.pdf (Accessed: 10.11.2014).